Hello, Hope!

Volume 3
Stories from Elder Orphan Care

Kim Jackson

Hello, Hope! Volume 3
Stories from Elder Orphan Care
© 2023 by Kim Jackson

Published by Elder Orphan Care Press
349-L Copperfield Blvd. Suite 211 Concord, NC 28025

ISBN: 979-8-3507-1136-3
Ebook: 979-8-3507-1137-0

Cover and interior design by Lisa Albinus, www.lisaalbinus.com
Proofreading by Sarah Seiz, www.littlelightshinebright.com
Copy editing by Karis Pratt, www.karisma-design.com

Printed in the United States of America
May 2023

To God be the glory!

Publish his glorious deeds among the nations.
Tell everyone about the amazing things he does.
Psalm 96:3 (NLT)

A Bit of Backstory

I felt an exhilarating rush of excitement as my church's mission leadership team spoke my name at God's throne of grace. My heart overflowed with gratitude as their voices joined together in prayer for me and the newly formed ministry called Elder Orphan Care.

After an enthusiastic amen, John put his hand on my shoulder. "Kim, I think God is saying, 'Fasten your seatbelt, it's going to be quite a ride!'"

A truer statement has never been made!

Looking back over the past twelve years, there's no doubt that it has been the adventure of a lifetime and continues to be so.

Thankfully I'm not alone on this ride. Each passing year more and more people come along on this journey to bring help and hope to older adults aging without adequate assistance, both in Romania and in North Carolina.

On September 18, 2010, the year before Elder Orphan Care came into existence, I wrote the following declaration in my journal. It's based on Romans 8:15 (MSG): "Today I choose to live with joyful expectancy, so I will greet God with a childlike, 'What's next, Papa?'"

I have quite an imagination, but never in my wildest dreams could I have envisioned what God had purposed. Just look at his faithfulness!

- Twelve years of serving alongside our Romanian ministry partners to care for hundreds of individuals who are elderly or frail

- Seven years of serving older adults in Cabarrus and Rowan counties of North Carolina

- Generous donors from twenty-two states investing in what God has commissioned us to do

- Funding from multiple grants, company matches, and support from nonprofit and business partnerships

- Our Safe and Loved at Home program that includes buddies who build relationships and groups who build ramps and do home modifications

- Volunteers in our Pantry and More program who shopped for and delivered thousands of pounds of groceries and supplies in 2022 alone

- Dozens of creative folks from all over the US who make and donate beautiful handmade items year after year

- Over 150 volunteers, aged two to ninety-two, who use their gifts to combat isolation, bring joy, and express God's love in an impressive range of ways

- Teams who travel from the US to Romania to offer practical assistance and communicate the love of God with over 500 older adults

- Annual holiday projects like Christmas Stockings of Joy, which deliver both presents and the gift of presence to nearly 1,000 older friends each year

- Intergenerational projects bringing young and old together for their mutual benefit

- Travels across the US to churches, camps and conventions presenting the work of EOC, creating partnerships, and encouraging individuals and groups to love their older neighbors

- Programs like our Summer Celebration and Winter Wonderland where our older friends gather for fun and fellowship

- Three full-time staff and the blessing of interns and fieldwork students from universities and colleges

- Lots of older adults coming to faith in Jesus in their later years

- Three volumes of *Hello, Hope!* in print. Who could have imagined?

I thank God for every victory and those on the way. And I am grateful for each person who played a part in making those successes reality.

If you are already a part of the Elder Orphan Care team, or if you're planning to join us, you may want to fasten *your* seatbelt because I believe some of our most magnificent miles are ahead of us!

God, teach me lessons for living so I can stay the course. Give me insight so I can do what you tell me—my whole life one long, obedient response. Guide me down the road of your commandments; I love traveling this freeway!
Psalm 119:33-35 (MSG)

Gratefully,

Kim Jackson

Elder Orphan Care Director

Concord, North Carolina

May 2023

The *Hello, Hope!* series shares the testimony of Elder Orphan Care in thirty brief, devotional stories. Volume 1 chronicles the birth and early days, and Volumes 2 and 3 continue our saga. All three volumes are available for purchase on Amazon.

Acknowledgements

Before they call I will answer;
while they are still speaking I will hear.
Isaiah 65:24

The first two volumes of *Hello, Hope!* were published thanks to the generosity of wonderful friends who chose to invest in sharing the stories of what God is doing through Elder Orphan Care.

I had barely begun to think of who might be led to do the same for this volume when a text and then a phone call made me aware and in awe that God had met the need even before I had asked!

May God abundantly reward the dear couple, who, when unexpected funds were given them, first thought of how they might use a portion to bless Elder Orphan Care and then chose to fund the publication of this book. We will honor their request to remain anonymous, giving God all the glory.

In the Beginning

And though your beginning was small,
your latter days will be very great.
Job 8:7 (ESV)

In the beginning...no, not *that* beginning! But the same Genesis God who so creatively birthed the universe and everything in it certainly was at work when three of his followers, 5,000 miles apart, unknowingly took actions that set their lives on a colossal collision course.

It was January 2006 in Romania. Viorel and Florica Pasca were innocently watching TV when they saw a startling news story about people who were elderly and homeless. Tragically, two had frozen to death on the streets of a nearby city. The story broke Viorel's and Florica's hearts. But it did more than that. It spurred them to action. Soon they traveled to find others who were old and without homes, speaking words that forever changed all their lives and, eventually, mine: "Come home with us."

In May 2008 I took a job at an assisted living community in North Carolina, even though my experience and education focused on youth. I was completely unaware that God would use that position to train me for what only he knew was coming next. I loved the residents of that community, but circumstances changed within two years to the degree that I began to cry out to God for a new adventure.

God used several friends to answer my prayers and reconnect me in 2010 with Andy Baker, president of Remember the Children. Despite the name of his ministry, Andy was helping the Pascas' ongoing mission to rescue people who were elderly and in need of shelter.

Fast forward to July, 2011 when our worlds converged. Viorel, Florica, Andy, and I sat together in Dumbrava, Romania, drinking incredibly strong coffee and sharing our passion to see abandoned elders valued and receiving care. Our partnership was born that day; what started out small has since grown in ways past what anyone could have envisioned. To date the Pascas have cared for over 2,500 individuals, and Elder Orphan Care has helped provide funds for food, care, medicines, shoes, buildings, Christmas gifts, and other needs, all shared with the love of God.

In 2017, due largely to friend and EOC staff person Tammy Blackburn's insight and energy, we began serving older adults aging alone in North Carolina, where EOC is based. Our local programs continue to grow rapidly, and since our world is aging faster than at any point in human history, the needs are increasing quickly as well.

Thanks to a connection made by our friends Zoli and Ema, EOC began partnering with another Romanian couple, Pastor Mircea and Dana Badea in 2018. The Badeas are currently caring for over one hundred elders who would otherwise be homeless.

Only God can bring a Romanian couple watching TV and a discouraged-but-praying American woman together across thousands of miles to do what he had planned for them before time began!

For that reason and so many more, I cannot think about the beginning days of EOC without remembering the truth of Ephesians 2:10: "For we are God's handiwork, created in Christ Jesus to do good works, which God prepared in advance for us to do."

Prayer

Dear God, I praise you! Your purposes are always being accomplished. Please show me the good works that you have planned for me to do today—and every day.

Return to Romania

My friends, we were kept from coming to you for a while,
but we never stopped thinking about you.
We were eager to see you and tried our best
to visit you in person.
1 Thessalonians 2:17 (CEV)

Nearly three years!

It seemed like an eternity since we were able to take an Elder Orphan Care team to Romania from the US. I had been traveling to Romania, where God birthed EOC, every year (and sometimes twice a year) since 2011. So, to be away for three years was nearly unbearable.

I kept in touch with our ministry partners there via phone calls, Skype, Facebook, and email, but nothing could replace being in Romania with them—our older friends, their care givers, and a multitude of brothers and sisters in Christ we have befriended over the years.

As much as I wanted a green light from God, it was clear it wasn't time to return yet. I like to imagine myself sitting at Jesus' feet to receive my personalized marching orders, so I kept praying, "Lord, when do you want us to return?" It became even more difficult when friends from other ministries began traveling back to Europe and asked us why we weren't going.

Late in the summer of 2022, I was in the shower when I sensed God's nudge to pray again about traveling to Romania. Suddenly it seemed that he wanted us to return in the fall! When I asked friends to pray, they all felt it was finally "a go from God" for a small team to make the trip. During our staff retreat we discussed several matters that needed to be handled before the trip could be finalized. Then everything fell into place.

On November 8, 2022, I stepped on Romanian soil for the first time since December 2019. It was wonderful to be reunited with our friends Zoli, Ema, and Brian, who had done so much so well for EOC in our absence.

When we arrived at the Pasca home, we saw Viorel looking out his window, pretending to be confused. "I think I know you," he teased. While we visited over coffee, he showed us a photograph taken one year ago to the day. It was an image of him in an ambulance being rushed to the hospital. His life had hung in the balance for months after that. We praised God together to witness his healing and to hear once again his enthusiastic "I have an idea!" and then tour the new independent living homes, one of his latest pioneering projects.

It was there that we were reunited with our friend Fanea. When I asked him how he liked living up on the hillside, his response was quick. "This is heaven on earth!"

Soon we saw more of our old friends hobbling toward us, holding in their gnarled hands treasured team photographs we'd given them on previous visits. People we'd never met welcomed us declaring, "We don't know you, but we've heard about you."

In room after crowded room we listened, prayed, and handed out special treats like bananas, bags of pufuleti (corn puffs), and Eugenias, their favorite cream cookies. We were greeted with hugs, multiple kisses on the cheek, and on several occasions, a beautiful song. "It's all I have to give you," they would state before singing their gift to us.

As we prepared to visit another room, we heard an excited voice calling out. Zoli explained that the woman had heard us outside her door and began shouting in Romanian, "Is it my children who have come? Have my children come for a visit?"

When we introduced ourselves as a team from the US, she asked, "Will you be traveling through Germany on your way home? Please tell my children hello."

Sitting down to visit with long-time friends Edith, Viorica, and Eleana was delightful. True to form, Eleana crocheted and Viorica peeled piles of carrots as we talked. And as is their gracious habit, we left with beautiful handmade gifts.

Mircea and Dana had asked if we might be able to provide winter shoes for the 102 elders in their care. We went from store to store in search of every available knock-off Croc-style shoe with a furry lining. When Veronica received her new shoes she exclaimed, "Oh these will be so warm for winter! Surely God has sent them to me!"

I've been told you shouldn't have favorites, but Irina found a special place in my heart from the moment I met her years ago. Our emotional reunion will forever be a highlight of my return to Romania, and I treasure the unique reminder of our friendship: a hat she knitted for me that matches the one she wears!

The gifts I receive in Romania come in many forms. Alexandru gave me one that can't be seen, worn, or displayed. Alexandru is blind, but he sees some matters more clearly than I do. I will always remember this dear man squeezing my hand and saying, "If we have faith, we have hope."

Prayer

Dear God, I thank you for directing my path, whether I travel near or far. Wherever you lead, help me to share the hope I have in you.

Lift Chair to Line Dancing

You have changed my sadness into a joyful dance; you have taken away my sorrow and surrounded me with joy.
Psalm 30:11 (GNT)

You would love Alma. She's feisty in the best sense of the word, full of faith in God, quick-witted, and determined.

I remember the first time I stepped into Alma's home in North Carolina. She sat on her couch, her legs swollen and weeping. Her doctor had said to keep her legs elevated, so she did the best she could by positioning a kitchen chair in front of her and putting her legs up on the seat. Thankfully EOC was able to provide Alma with a lift chair, which made a world of difference.

Any time after that, when I would come for a visit and remark on that beautiful burgundy lift chair, she would respond in true Alma form, "Don't you even think about sitting in my chair!"

Not long after I met Alma, she was hospitalized for six days. She was told her heart had a leaky valve which would need repair. Alma faced that news by looking to God. Her prayer was simple. "Lord, I know that you can heal that leak, and I'm asking you to do it." And he did!

Alma is intentional in partnering with the Lord for her health. And she won't allow us to pamper her, even when we take her to an appointment: "Don't let me out at the door, just park the car," she'll direct. "I can walk!"

That sort of determination has served Alma well over the years as she cared for her son who had developmental challenges. She gave him the very best life possible, despite a few naysayers. Her faith carried her through her husband's death, and then her son's not long afterwards. She's resolved to live independently despite issues with low vision.

There are so many reasons to admire Alma, and I've added one more to the list. This one has to do with a class she attends at the YMCA. She invited me to come, and I accepted.

I spotted her immediately in the room filled with participants wearing leggings and T-shirts.

Line dancing! Alma was line dancing! Watching her scoot, shuffle, and kick, I nearly broke into a happy dance myself!

Several friends gathered around Alma during a break, and I was able to tell them how proud I was to see her choosing to be active.

"I used to lift Alma's legs into the car when I picked her up for appointments," Sadie recalled. "Now look at her!"

Theresa, one of the leaders, joined the conversation. I asked how she got involved in line dancing. "I met a woman who was ninety-two and she was dancing, so I decided I could too!"

Another woman tapped her leg. "I have issues with my knee, so I just do what I can and have fun!"

"Move it or lose it," someone else chimed in. "Motion is lotion," I agreed.

"I wish more of our people would come to these classes," Alma lamented. "Some of them sit in front of the TV all day long. That's not good."

The music started up and everyone returned to their places on the gym floor. I stood by Alma doing my best to follow the instructor's directions.

Alma looked my way in between scoots and kicks and said with a grin, "Hope you can keep up with me!"

Prayer

Dear God, I give you praise for the health I have, and I ask that you show me specific ways that I can stay as active as possible for all the days you have planned for me.

Seven-Day Church

*Whatever you do, work heartily, as for the Lord and not
for men, knowing that from the Lord you will receive the
inheritance as your reward. You are serving the Lord Christ.*
Colossians 3:23-24 (ESV)

The dictionary defines *church* as a building for public, and especially Christian, worship.

But the biblical definition of *church* is the body of Christ, believers who have accepted Jesus' gift of salvation.

The church is so much more than a building!

Our ministry partner in Romania, Pastor Mircea, has a unique perspective on this topic. If you ask him about his occupation, he will reply, "The kingdom of God is my job." Then he will add, "I serve the seven-day church."

When asked to explain, he's happy to do so.

> Of course, the church must meet; believers, the body of Christ must come together. But then we must go out: Monday, Tuesday, Wednesday! We all must "do the do" and not just talk the talk. We are the church walking through the village; the people may not come to our building, but we are the church they experience. The seven-day church is a Monday-through-Sunday, living, breathing church.

> For me, every day is a preaching day. My sermon may be fixing the gate of a widow's home or planting vegetables in the garden. God has asked us to care for one hundred old people who have no one else to love them. We care for them at all times. That is church.

> I call the path that runs between the buildings where the elderly live "Jesus Street." We put "Jesus Lives Here" signs on the doors. Every day as I walk down Jesus Street I see people in need of comfort, encouragement, a smile. They must know they still have a role; they are needed, they

are a full person. Some of them still need to know the Lord.

We are able to provide for them because God is great. He has provided from the start. Here is one story that tells of his greatness.

I was at the hospital visiting and began praying for the patient I knew. A woman at the end of the hallway heard me praying and asked her son to find me. She asked me to pray for her, too. We talked for some time. I shared the Lord with her and she received Jesus into her life. I give God the glory.

Months later I traveled to another city for a conference. I had been fasting, but I felt the Spirit tell me to go to a restaurant and eat. I had very little money, so I decided to buy the cheapest meal, which was biscuits and water. But a man tapped me on the shoulder and said, "Remember me? Come to my table." I realized it was the son of the woman I had prayed for and brought to salvation.

I asked, "How is your mother?"

He replied, "She has died in the Lord, but I felt I would see you again and when I did, I knew I was to ask, 'How is that church that functions from Monday through Sunday? How is that seven-day church you are building, the one where elders who have no one are cared for every day?'"

And then I was surprised to hear him tell me, "I will help you build it."

Mircea concludes his story with a smile. "And he did. But that's a story for another day!"

During my last visit to Romania Pastor Mircea told me he encourages himself with this verse from Galatians 6:9: "Let us not become weary in doing good, for at the proper time we will reap a harvest if we do not give up."

There are challenges, to be sure, because Pastor Mircea's and Dana's service to God is not contained to a few hours in a building on Sunday mornings. Theirs is a seven-day church.

Prayer

Dear God, I thank you for this inspiration.
Please show me more ways to make the
seven-day church a reality in my life.

Lightbulb Love

Let your light so shine before men, that they may see
your good works and glorify your Father in heaven.
Matthew 5:16 (NKJV)

Have you ever stood on a step ladder to change a lightbulb? Depending on your balance, the safety precautions you take, and your level of common sense, that simple task can be either a piece of cake or a disaster in the making.

According to the National Institute for Occupational Safety and Health, each year in the US more than 500,000 people are treated for and about 300 people die from ladder-related injuries.[1]

Given those statistics, you can be sure we are glad when an EOC client calls to ask us to change a lightbulb rather than finding that person on the floor at the base of a ladder after unsuccessfully attempting it on their own.

But we would be even happier if a caring neighbor, a church friend, or someone else stopped by for a visit and noticed that person sitting in the dark and offered to put in a new lightbulb for them right then.

We love to hear stories from our older friends with limited mobility who tell us about neighbors who come by each week on their way to work to roll their cumbersome trashcans to the curb and then send their teenager over in the evening to retrieve the container and pull it back up the driveway for them.

Such simple acts of love are so helpful to someone unable to accomplish them on their own.

A few summers ago, I had the privilege of spending two months in Indiana at Wonder Valley Christian Camp telling hundreds of campers of all ages about Elder Orphan Care.

---

1 Peter Simeonov, PhD, and Sydney Webb, PhD, "It's National Ladder Safety Month," NIOSH Science Blog, March 13, 2017, https://blogs.cdc.gov/niosh-science-blog/2017/03/13/ladder-safety-month/.

I encouraged them to love their older neighbors, not just when they have a need, but as a matter of daily living.

Hopefully some of what I taught "stuck." But there's no doubt that what I learned from them continues to impact my life. Each week I would ask a different age group of campers to create what I call a "Love Your Older Neighbor Alphabet of Action." Here are some of their responses that I compiled.

I love these ideas!

Adopt them into your heart; always say hello; ask to sit on the porch with them.

Be kind; bake cookies with them; bring my dog to visit.

Change lightbulbs; create crafts together; call them.

Donate items they need; do a good deed; drink tea together.

Eat a meal with them; encourage them; entertain with fun skits.

Fix broken things; follow their good example; fish together.

Garden with them; give gifts; go grocery shopping.

Hug them; help with pets; hear their stories.

Ice removal in winter; invite them to church; invent adaptive equipment.

Join them at special events; jigsaw puzzles together; joke with them nicely.

Know their likes; knit with them; keep them safe.

Listen to their stories; love them like grandparents; learn a skill from them.

Mow their yard; make them laugh; make a special recipe together.

Notice them; never give up on them; need their advice.

Organize their pantry; open doors for them; offer to teach technology.

Pray for them; polish fingernails; put their Christmas decorations up.

Question them about their faith; quilt with them; quit judging them.

Respect them; read with them; recall memories together.

Sing with them; smile at them; spend time together.

Take their garbage out; tell them about Jesus; try something new together.

Understand them; unscrew tight lids on jars; uproot weeds for them.

Visit them; vacuum for them; value them.

Watch TV together; wait for them; write them a letter.

"X"cited to be together; "X"ample, be a good one; "X"tra things done for them.

Yard work assistance; yogurt frozen treats to share; yes to help.

Zip their coat; zoo trip together; zealously share God's love.

Prayer

Dear God: I thank you for young people and the insights they have to offer. Please direct me to a specific idea from the list that I can do with an older friend, perhaps asking a younger friend to join me.

Biggest Place on the Map

But as it is, they desire a better country, that is,
a heavenly one. Therefore God is not ashamed to be called
their God, for he has prepared for them a city.
Hebrews 11:16 (ESV)

There was a time long ago when the population of heaven was not personal to me. But now when I think of those I love who are in the presence of Jesus, the list is long. It will only grow longer.

In the past few months, I have attended several funerals, spoken at a few, and returned to Romania after three years to discover that many of my older friends had died in my absence. Friends like Georgetta, who had become a child of God at age seventy and who repeated her testimony with grateful tears each time we visited. I'll always remember her grabbing my hands and pulling me into the room she shared with three others to point once again at her baptismal certificate on the wall. Imagine—now Georgetta is with her Jesus!

I think of Paul, who was desperate to end his life on earth, but who eventually chose eternal life in Christ and lived joyfully until death transported him into the very presence of Jesus!

Randy Alcorn calls death "a heartbreaking interruption." So, although we grieve our believing friends' deaths, we can say with confident joy, "See you later, Georgetta, Paul, and Joseph!" "Goodbye for now, Irene, Patricia, JoAnn, and Walter!" "Catch up with you soon, Ed, Mrs. Potter, Kenny, and Cathy!"

All these interruptions in sweet relationships reminds me of a booklet I have called *Pell's Notes*, dated July 1911. I love how the unnamed writer speaks of heaven:

> You have heard of Brownsville all your life. But Brownsville never meant anything to you until a year ago when a loved one went there to live. Now the mere mention of the name sends

the blood rushing to your heart. Brownsville? Why, Brownsville is everything to you now. Before it was a mere name: now it is the biggest place on the map.

You pass over the big headlines in the morning paper to find the little news items from Brownsville at the bottom of the column on the last page. Jones died in Brownsville yesterday. They have begun to pave the street in Brownsville. Mrs. Smith, of Brownsville, gave a dinner and your son was there! What an interesting place is Brownsville! And it all came about because a loved one went to Brownsville to live a year ago.

So you have heard of the other world—the unseen world—all your life, but it never meant anything to you until the other day when a loved one went there to live. And at last heaven is real to you. Before it was a mere name. Now it is the biggest place, the most interesting place on the map of the universe. Every time you hear heaven mentioned the blood goes rushing to your heart. You have a vital connection with heaven now; you feel that you have a part and lot in it. And it is all because your loved one—a part of yourself—has gone there to live.

Oh, dear friends! Let's be sure to meet one day *in heaven*, the "Brownsville" God has planned for us!

Prayer

Dear Jesus, I thank you for preparing a place for me (John 14:2-3) and providing the way for me to get there (John 14:6). Lord, I pray that I may show many others the way there, too!

It Never Occurred to Me

Teach us to number our days,
that we may gain a heart of wisdom.
Psalm 90:12

I was walking down a long flight of stairs at the front of a church after giving a presentation about Elder Orphan Care. A gray-haired gentleman was exiting parallel to me, using the well-worn ramp to navigate his walker to the parking lot.

He stopped, so I did too. Turning to me, he spoke wistfully, "I built this ramp twenty years ago. It never occurred to me that one day I would need to use it." I've pondered that statement time and time again.

I doubt that you are growing younger, and I know for sure I'm not. When I was young, I thought people in their sixties were ancient. Now that I am sixty-six, my perspective has changed! Aging is not negotiable, whether you're nine or ninety. And yet we often act as if aging will pass us by and there will be no issues. Good luck with that!

I'm a baby boomer and many of my friends have retired. Some have built what they call their dream homes. I want to rejoice with them, yet I cringe when I see steps leading to the front porch, realize all bedrooms are on the second floor, or see other designs that are not particularly well thought out. I know that one broken hip or some other type of health issue might very well prohibit them from being able to enter that home let alone live in it long term.

Most people don't like to think about aging, and yet the only other option is death. Someone has noted that most people spend more time planning for a yearly vacation than they do for their retirement years, or, more importantly, for where they will spend eternity.

As I age, I am understanding more and more that I rarely have control in every situation, but I do, in many cases, have choices. Since I am growing older like everyone else, I have made the choice to ponder, plan and prepare as much as is in my ability, so that I might make the most of every day God gives me.

Here are a few suggestions:

- Commit to some type of appropriate exercise plan with a functional fitness focus.

- Make wise food choices.

- Prepare your will and other end-of-this-life plans.

- Practice doing everyday tasks using your non-dominant hand.

- Spend time in God's Word, in prayer, and in worship.

- Make and take time to have fun.

- Take a critical look at your home's design and make modifications before they're needed.

- Develop new friendships and strengthen old friendships.

- Use the gifts God has given you.

- Learn a new hobby, skill, or language to benefit brain health.

- Encourage and serve others.

- Determine to be grateful.

I am sure there will be many circumstances forthcoming in my life which, like the gentleman I met outside the church, never occurred to me. I have no idea the quantity or quality of days God has written in his book for me, but I will do what I can—and you can, too—in choosing to make those days the best they can be.

Prayer

Dear Lord, I thank you for every never-before-never-again day you give me. Please direct me in the choices I can make to live each day for your glory.

Presents and Presence

So if you sinful people know how to give good gifts to your children, how much more will your heavenly Father give good gifts to those who ask him.
Matthew 7:11 (NLT)

Which do you prefer: Gifts or a visit? Presents or presence?

I would venture to guess that the answer is *both*.

It's nice when presents somehow appear on the front porch or we receive a surprise anonymous gift. But how much better when the presents are accompanied by the presence of someone connected to the gift?

Each November we give our older friends in North Carolina a wish list to fill out. The form guides them in listing ideas for gifts that they want or need, plus favorite colors, and foods.

Our staff takes that information and creates tags that are distributed to churches and businesses, who then place them on their Christmas trees. Kind and generous people take the tags, purchase gifts, and return them to us for our volunteers to wrap. Other volunteers deliver the presents, along with their presence, one very special day in December.

When this program first began, we had a smaller group of clients and not nearly as many volunteers, so my colleague Tammy did a lot of the work. She says that at that time it was difficult to get our older friends to put much of anything on their lists. For whatever reasons, a few of them couldn't dream for gifts beyond fuzzy socks! Thankfully that has changed.

I am so glad our friends have begun asking for gifts they really desire. Imagine the joy when Wilma, who has advanced degrees in music education and who taught private piano lessons for years, humbly asked for and then received— thanks to a kind and generous donor—a weighted keyboard! Now music is once again filling her home with the additional benefits of increased dexterity, decreased anxiety, and the potential for improved concentration and memory!

Tammy tells this sweet story about another special gift:

> At first, I had to coax Etheline to give me any ideas at all for her Christmas Wish List. Finally, she chose pajamas. I asked her favorite color and that's when she said she would love more than anything to have a pair of red pajamas. So I made it my goal to find her the perfect pair of red pajamas!
>
> I looked at all the usual stores where pajamas were affordable, but with no success. I decided to go to the Belk store even though I knew how expensive they would be. As I walked through the doors, I prayed for a pair of red pajamas. And there they were on a table at the front of the store! A beautiful pair of red pajamas with white polka dots, and in her size. And they were 60% off that day!

Etheline loves those pajamas! When we visit it's not unusual to find her wearing them as her favorite lounge clothes, which can be confirmed by her photograph on the cover of this book!

In Romania our gift-giving looks a bit different, but the joy is universal. The gifts we deliver most always have an impact that far exceeds the size or cost of the present. One of our Romanian elder friends, who is blind, touched every gift in his Christmas Stocking of Joy, then held up the winter socks and ran his hands over them, feeling their warmth. "Oh, these are good quality!" he declared.

When Christmas Stockings of Joy are hand delivered to our friends in Romania, they often gratefully receive the stocking, but then motion to a spot next to them, inviting us to sit, because for them, visiting is a treasured gift as well.

We frequently hear, "Thank you! May God be praised! I have found many wonderful things inside this stocking!"

But we also hear, "Please come back, even if you don't bring us anything."

Presents and presence. Both can be gifts from God.

Prayer

*Dear Lord: I thank you for your gifts that come
in such a variety of packages, both tangible and
intangible. Please increase my gratitude for even the
smallest present I receive while reminding me that my
presence may be the most important gift I can give.*

If You Ask God

I cry out to God Most High,
to God who fulfills his purpose for me.
Psalm 57:2 (ESV)

He sits in a camping chair on the church parking lot from 9:00 a.m. to 11:00 a.m. The sign posted in front of him, close to the well-traveled road, asks, "MAY I PRAY FOR YOU?" on one side and declares, "YOU HAVE JUST BEEN PRAYED FOR" on the other.

I've driven by this scene several times, thinking it a bit curious, but glad to see someone offering to pray, and in fact, praying. Sometimes I've wondered what this man's story might be. But I've never stopped.

Till today.

Well, not at first. I drove past as I have before, but this time I felt a nudge, the Spirit of God prompting me to turn around and go back.

I did.

When I pulled in, he rose to greet me. He asked my name and how he could pray for me.

I asked his name. He's Larry. I don't know his age, but he has a rim of silver hair and the face of someone who has weathered more than a few years.

I asked him to pray for Elder Orphan Care. I told him how God has been faithful to grow EOC over the years from our start in Romania to our service with older adults in North Carolina. I shared some of the needs of our Romanian friends, and the waiting list of older adults in North Carolina who would benefit from what we do if we had more resources. I told him about a couple of the big dreams we continue to put before the Lord.

Larry listened. He asked, "Why Romania?" "Where does your

funding come from?" We talked a while longer and then he took my hands in his and prayed.

His prayer was simple, tender, powerful. The noise of the traffic rushing by caused me to lean in close to hear each word as Larry asked for God's abundant provision for EOC. Several times he paused, and although my eyes were closed, I knew he was crying.

I know Larry is the pray-er, but I couldn't help myself. I prayed for Larry.

After our "amens" he let go of my hands and pulled a handkerchief from his back pocket to wipe the tears from his face. "I don't know why you've affected me like this."

I smiled. "Maybe it's because you have God's heart. He's quite fond of Elder Orphan Care."

I thanked him again and started toward my car. But then I stopped and turned around for a second time. "Larry, why do you do this?"

"Oh, I've been doing peculiar things for thirty years."

"But why this?"

"I asked God," Larry replied matter-of-factly. "And if you ask God, he'll give you something to do. He told me to pray."

"I'm so glad you accepted God's assignment, Larry. You've encouraged me today and I'm certain that what you do makes God smile."

"Well, I don't know about that."

I gently disagreed. "I do."

Prayer

Dear God, I know that as long as I have a pulse, I have a purpose. Please continue showing me what you would have me do, day by day. I'll be listening.

Duck Eggs to Donor

*And my God will meet all your needs according
to the riches of his glory in Christ Jesus.*
Philippians 4:19

Janna Syester's mom, Pat, was wild about the homemade
ice cream Janna makes, and who wouldn't be? We all agreed
it put store-bought ice cream to shame. One day a neighbor
helped her with a project and wouldn't accept any payment,
but he did mention that the next time Janna made ice cream
he wouldn't mind if she gave some to him!

No one could have imagined that Janna's ice cream could
improve. That is, until one day she decided to use duck eggs
instead of chicken eggs in her recipe.

Goodness! How could that ice cream become even more delish?
I can tell you from personal experience that ice cream made with
duck eggs rates a fourteen on a scale of one to ten! Janna's mom
agreed, and it became clear that she was pretty sure she should
have it for dessert every night of the week.

Consequently, Janna needed to have lots of duck eggs on hand,
which was not necessarily easy to accomplish. So she posted this
on Facebook: "Does anyone know someone who sells duck eggs
in the Concord, NC, area?"

Several people replied, including Robin, who suggested a former
boss and friend of hers named Jerry.

The connection was made, and Janna began driving a few miles
to Jerry's farm each week to pick up duck eggs. Her mom often
rode along, enjoying the Sunday afternoon outing. At first the
trips were more of a task to accomplish, but conversations began
to deepen with Jerry and soon they became friends.

Janna was the chair of the EOC board at the time, and has since
come on staff, so as their friendship grew it was natural for her to
tell stories about sharing God's love with older adults locally and
in Romania. Jerry, being a good listener and a follower of Christ,

was touched by what God does through Elder Orphan Care. He let Janna know he was praying and always had a Scripture verse or encouraging word for her.

One Sunday afternoon when Janna got home from Farmer Jerry's, she opened the carton and found not only eggs, but a check made out to Elder Orphan Care!

What a win-win-win! Thanks to Jerry's duck eggs, Pat enjoyed decadent ice cream, a friendship was born, and Elder Orphan Care was blessed with a new donor!

Janna's mom is feasting in the presence of Jesus these days, so Janna reserves her homemade ice cream for special occasions. But each week Janna still drives to Jerry's farm to get eggs and stays to visit a bit. And the first of each month, tucked inside an egg carton, is Jerry's donation to Elder Orphan Care.

Prayer

Dear God, I thank you for how you creatively bring people together for your purposes. Lord, help me to take time to get to know the people you have placed around me so I can encourage them and receive encouragement as well.

Don't These People Have Any Kids?

Learn to do good. Seek justice. Help the oppressed.
Defend the cause of orphans. Fight for the rights of widows.
Isaiah 1:17 (NLT)

A man stopped at our mission conference booth and read the words *Elder Orphan Care* in large letters on our display, then took a cursory glance at the photographs of some of the older friends we help. Stepping back, he shook his head incredulously and spouted, "Don't these people have any kids to take care of them?"

I won't be able to tell you if he said anything else or if any of us at the booth responded. I was in shock. Might still be. Could he be serious? Think about it:

I'm in my sixties and have never married. I have no children.

Sadly, three of our dear North Carolina clients' children died in the past year. They *had* children...

One of our North Carolina clients has a very caring daughter, but she lives quite a distance away. When her mother had a medical emergency, she wasn't available to help.

When I first visited Viorel and Florica Pasca in Romania to learn about their ministry with elderly people who were abandoned, I assumed the elders they cared for did not have children. Was I ever wrong! Most of them do have children, but for a variety of reasons, they are as alone in the world as if they'd never had offspring.

Viorel reflects,

> "I have learned and seen over the years that anything can happen to anyone, that no one can have the security of a peaceful and carefree old age, that family or loved ones are not always a guarantee of a pleasant sunset in life.

> Neither position in society nor money can be things that you can be sure will ensure you a clear sky in the years to come. Businesspeople, intellectuals, a judge, professors,

accountants, and others have been brought to us who would never have thought that life would be so unpredictable and yet, the pain of losing a business, home, or health cannot be compared to the suffering and drama experienced by those abandoned by those closest to them."

Unfortunately, just because a person has children doesn't guarantee that those children will be able or willing to assist them. It's been our experience that while some children are helping their parents in every way possible, others have their own health or other issues, or don't seem to care at all. A few seem to have an almost evil agenda and say and do things that are thoroughly self-centered. Some are geographically removed while others may live close by but are altogether distant emotionally. Frequently we discover that parents and their children have had major conflicts throughout their lifetimes that remain unresolved.

We can confirm that while there are two sides to every story, often we only hear the aging parent's side. That story might be communicated through the lens of hurt, trauma, miscommunication, or failing memory. Thankfully we have seen some victories where reconciliation has begun; communication has been restored, and burdens lifted. We pray for more scenarios like those.

I must be careful not to judge. When my mom suffered a major medical crisis, I had the ability and the desire to relocate from Florida to Illinois to help care for her. I have many friends who have made major, life-changing decisions to be able to assist their aging family members. Every situation is unique, no doubt, and not everyone can do what my friends and I have done or are doing.

Still, the Bible seems clear in this regard. In Exodus 20:12 we read the fifth commandment which begins, "Honor your father and your mother," a theme that's repeated elsewhere, including the powerful statement made in 1 Timothy 5:8: "Anyone who does not provide for their relatives, and especially for their own household, has denied the faith and is worse than an unbeliever."

Unfortunately (if you understand my meaning), I have job security as the director of Elder Orphan Care. There will always be older adults aging alone. I cannot become the biological child who helps take care of that aging parent or the relative who comes alongside an older adult who is a true orphan.

But I am a child of God, and that alone motivates me to care for those people, blood relation or not, who find themselves aging without the support needed to not only survive but thrive.

Prayer

Dear Lord, you know my specific circumstances. Whether I am in need of care as I age or am able to care for those aging around me, please provide what I need.

What We've Heard Lately

Words have power in matters of life and death,
and those who love them will savor their fruit.
Proverbs 18:21 (VOICE)

The following statements made by our older friends in Romania and North Carolina speak volumes. I think they have a power all their own. And I've included a couple that might make you giggle.

"You deliver my groceries, but you bring me joy!"

"I would like a CD player that plays continuously so I can listen to the Bible all night long."

"You really got me everything on that grocery list? I can't believe it!"

"Now I know there really are 'people angels.'"

"So I'm a part of the Elder Orphan Care club now? You all are going to help take care of me? That makes me feel like I'm wrapped up in a blanket in my momma's arms."

"I had a lovely group of volunteers from Elder Orphan Care install a handicap ramp for me so I can get in and out of the house by myself. I am so excited! It really is a nice, solid ramp."

"I could have only dreamed of ever having a coat like this."

"Are the winter hats coming?"

"Are the new calendars coming?"

"My friend in Indiana sends me cards at just the right time. I was depressed so I was having a little pity party for myself, and then I got Carol's card. I felt so much better."

"All this for me? I'm overwhelmed!"

"I don't think my Edna Insurance pays for that. I'm switching to United Way."

"I am so happy I could just cry."

"I've seen things like this on TV, but now it's me getting the big surprise!"

"Of course I'm happy! You said you'd come back, and you did!"

"I like the painting on the front of the card I received from my EOC friend in Indiana yesterday. The scripture included in the card is very encouraging."

"I don't like that 'zoom' class but I'm going to try one of those 'yogurt' classes at the YMCA."

"Sometimes I have to just encourage myself, so I sang 'How Great Thou Art' right there in the foyer of the rehab facility!"

"Thank you for not forgetting us even when you could not come to us."

"I don't want this gathering to end."

"When all of you are here I feel as if I am surrounded by angels."

"I went to my first strictly social event in nearly twenty years. It was a Winter Wonderland party, an Elder Orphan Care event. It was so much fun. I can't remember when I've laughed so hard and so much. I sat at a table with some really fun ladies. I am hoping to be able to see them again. I am so grateful transportation was arranged so I could attend."

"Our talk revived my spirit."

"I've never felt so loved."

"God has not left us as orphans."

Prayer

Dear Lord, I thank you for reminding me that every action I take, every service I render, and every word I speak can have a positive impact. Please show me a new way I might encourage someone today.

Something Didn't Feel Right

I will instruct you and teach you in the way you should go;
I will counsel you with my loving eye on you.
Psalm 32:8

A friend told me about an experience she had which impacted me on several levels. I believe it's a story worth sharing with people who care about older adults aging alone. Here's the story, in her words:

> As I pulled in my driveway that evening I glanced across the street. Normally at that time of the day I would see my neighbor's TV flickering through the sheer curtains on her front windows, but there were no lights on at all. I also realized I hadn't seen her car move in a couple of days. Something felt different, but when I asked another neighbor, he assured me he had seen Ms. M outside earlier, so I put my concern away.

> Even though we've lived across the street from one another for thirty-six years, it was when Ms. M's husband and son both died within a year that I began to pay closer attention to her, knowing that now she was completely alone. My husband and I invited her out to eat with us on occasion and we had more frequent visits when I went to my mailbox and she was in her yard.

> I left at 6:30 a.m. the next morning to help with an event at my church. I finished around 10:00 a.m. and planned to get a few other things done before going home. But as I drove, I felt compelled to check on my neighbor. I hadn't consciously thought of her all morning, but now I felt an urgency to see if Ms. M was OK. So instead of turning right to do my errands, I drove straight instead, heading home. Something didn't feel right. I needed to check on my neighbor.

> I knocked on her door, but she didn't respond for a few minutes. When she did, I could tell she was disoriented.

"Ms. M, are you feeling OK?"

"No, I think not."

"Then I would like to take you to the emergency room."

"Yes, I think so, yes, I think that's a good idea."

After an examination and tests, the doctor shook his head, "You got here just in time. It's sepsis."

I'm confident that my friend saved her neighbor's life that day. She paid attention, noticed changes in patterns, cared enough to get involved. She was led by a nudge from the Spirit of God and she obeyed. Her neighbor is alive because she did.

When I thanked my friend for sharing this story, she gave additional insight:

I believe God was ahead of that moment; preparing me to know her better, to pay attention, to know her patterns so it would get my attention when something changed.

One of the big tendencies in our world is to keep facing forward, to mind our own business, but what I am learning is that to know others and be known by them is what God desires.

Prayer

Dear God, which of my neighbors are you asking me to get to know better? I want to know them and then be prepared to assist them if the need arises. I pray they would do the same for me.

Romans 8:28 in Action

*We are assured and know that [God being a partner
in their labor] all things work together and are [fitting
into a plan] for good to and for those who love God
and are called according to [His] design and purpose.*
Romans 8:28 (AMPC)

Like so many "God things," we didn't see it coming.

We hatched a plan called Christmas Stockings of Joy in 2016 to modify our holiday outreach in Romania, putting less emphasis on what we could buy in the US and ship, and prioritizing what we could buy in Romania to fill hundreds of stockings with gifts.

That is, until 2020. Early on we realized we would not be taking a Christmas Stockings of Joy team from the US that year. As I communicated that fact with our dear friends Zoli and Ema in Romania, I quickly realized if the Christmas project was going to happen for hundreds of our older friends, they would need to take on that responsibility.

It made sense, and they were more than qualified. Having served alongside our team for four years, they knew the drill. When I asked Zoli and Ema if they would take on the challenge, their response was precious and powerful: "We would be honored to be the hands and feet of EOC."

And hands and feet they were! Thanks to them, our dear friends received all their fun, practical, and delicious items, along with the new calendars from the Romanian Bible Society and the handmade hats and scarves that were shipped from the US—all gifts they await with excitement each year. Romans 8:28 was in full force.

In 2021 we still didn't feel the Lord leading us to travel to Romania. So, all things worked together for good again, and Zoli, Ema, their son Brian, and volunteers they recruited worked hard to once again plan, shop, pack, and deliver hundreds of Christmas Stockings of Joy to our older friends in over twenty humble care homes in half a dozen rural villages.

Janna, Ellen, and I were finally able to travel to Romania in the fall of 2022, but it was too early for Christmas Stockings of Joy. In December Zoli, Ema, and their crew put their well-oiled machine to work, ordering hundreds of water bottles (such a gift for those living in care homes with no running water in their rooms), getting photos printed, buying devotional books, finding best prices on socks, fruit, treats, and notebooks, and scheduling volunteers to pack all those items in the handmade stockings we had shipped, along with squeeze balls (a type of physical therapy), four-color ink pens, small plush animals, and 500 handcrafted Christmas cards. No small feat!

Thanks to their labors of love, our dear ones received all their Christmas presents, along with the presence of Zoli, Ema, and a team of Romanian volunteers.

When we Skyped to evaluate how it had gone, Zoli and Ema excitedly told me their stories. Somewhere in the middle of our conversation I had an epiphany. I realized there was probably never going to be a need for us to send a team to Romania at Christmas time. Zoli and Ema had put processes in place, recruited volunteers, and completed the project with excellence. Why would we travel to Romania to do what they were doing so well?

I must admit I will miss being a part of the Christmas Stockings of Joy project in Romania. But as I asked Zoli and Ema to tell me some of the outcomes they've seen as this process has unfolded, it was further confirmation that God had taken what seemed to be a problem and turned it to a blessing.

Here are some of their insights:

It's wonderful to see young and old become a team and work together, using their unique spiritual gifts.

We have noticed that while other groups may bring some gifts, few spend time listening, smiling, and talking to the elders. Like the EOC teams from the US, we make this a priority.

Elders like for someone to listen to them, as they have so many life stories to share.

We have begun to see young people getting involved and understand how important their work is and how they can make a difference. For a few days, a grandma brought her eight- and ten-year-old grandsons to help pack and deliver the gifts to the elders. The young boys, even though they were tired, insisted that they wanted to come help pack and deliver the next day too. Setting up an example empowers the young ones; thus the ministry continues, and God is glorified and souls are joyful.

Ministering to the elders together with the church members has helped us become better friends and prayer partners. Serving the elders helps people who didn't think they can do anything become aware of the person next to them and consider how they can help. In many ways their own soul benefits as well.

We rejoice that we can be living examples of Romans 10:15: "How beautiful are the feet of those who bring good news!"

Prayer

Dear God, I am grateful that you are all-knowing, and you ultimately fit everything together in ways that are best, whether I can understand it at the time or not. I recommit to trusting you to work all things together for my good.

On the Road Again

"Go in peace," the priest replied.
"For the Lord is watching over your journey."
Judges 18:6 (NLT)

It was a beautiful November evening, and the music was blaring on my car's stereo as I traveled south on I-75. I'd spoken about Elder Orphan Care at a church in Indiana earlier that day and was feeling encouraged but a bit weary. I began thinking about stopping in Kentucky to stay overnight on my way home to North Carolina.

And I did stop . . . abruptly . . . but nowhere near a hotel.

A deer leaping on to the interstate provided the reason I slammed my brakes so suddenly that the semitrailer truck following too closely behind my compact car couldn't stop in time to avoid a bone rattling collision. The impact launched my car into the air. It flipped three times before landing.

I wasn't counting. The eyewitnesses shared that information when they found me—alive—much to their surprise. When I eventually got to look at what was left of my car (not much) I was overwhelmed with gratitude.

No doubt I should be dead. God obviously had a different idea. And so, twelve years later, I am healthy and happy, and with many miles behind me as I've continued to travel to share about EOC and brag on God.

A deer and a semi destroyed my leased vehicle. That gave God even more opportunity to remind me of his faithfulness. Let's just say that I wasn't at the height of my financial stability at that time. In other words, no car salesman in their right mind would sell me a vehicle.

So I wrote this in my journal: "Dear God: I need a car, and I'd like a story, too!"

Six weeks after the accident, still dependent on loaner cars and rides from friends, I got a call from Nancy at my church explaining that someone had donated a car and I could have it! It was December 23, and we all agreed the car was a God-provided Christmas gift, so a plan was quickly set in motion for me to meet the family at the Department of Motor Vehicles to sign over the title before they closed for the holidays. Drama ensued in the crush to complete the transaction by 5:00 p.m., but at 4:55 p.m. I not only had new friends, I had the title for a 1995 Pontiac Bonneville that I dubbed "Bonnie the Christmas Car."

She was sixteen years old and had more than a few issues, but I was grateful to be on the road again.

When I drove Bonnie over 500 miles to Florida to speak at a woman's retreat, the "check engine" light kept me company all the way—ironically, it was the only light on the dash that worked!

Glenda, one of the women there who heard me share how God answered my prayer for both a car and a story, wrote this poem:

Ode to Bonnie

O thank you, God, for Bonnie—

She is my Christmas car.

Each time I sit behind the wheel

She reminds me who You are!

The God who knows my every need

Before I even ask . . .

You're with me everywhere I go,

Through each and every task.

Please let my life be a pattern of

A God who takes my load;

And Lord, keep me and Bonnie safe

As we roll along life's road!

Bonnie lasted about a year before parts began to fall off with frequency and the headlights and taillights quit working entirely. But God's provision continued when in 2013 friends Michael and Gail sent out an email with the subject line "Kim Needs a Set of Wheels." Friends gave generously, and in yet another amazing story, I got a car! I ordered a "FRNDMBL" personalized license plate to honor the twenty-seven friends and three churches who provided a way for me to return to the road.

Currently I'm driving EllaBell, a fifteen-year-old Honda Element. Yes, she has a story too! She's the perfect EOC-mobile, can haul wheelchairs and people and twelve twenty-seven gallon containers of supplies for shipment to Romania, though not all at the same time!

I'm hoping EllaBell will last another fifteen years, but most of all I am grateful to still be traveling the road God directs me to take, no matter what vehicle he provides.

Prayer

Dear God: I thank you for the magnitude and multitude of ways you provide for me. Please show me a specific way today that I may be able to provide for someone's need.

Help Opens the Door

May the God of hope fill you with all joy and peace
as you trust in him, so that you may overflow
with hope by the power of the Holy Spirit.
Romans 15:13

It was my first-time delivering groceries to Rayma. When I knocked on her apartment door, it opened just enough for an arm to extend toward me.

"Hello, it's Kim with Elder Orphan Care."

There was no response. So I hung the grocery bag on her arm, which disappeared and then reappeared! I repeated the process with two more bags, and then the door shut. I never saw her face or heard her voice.

Granted, it was 2020 and the height of the pandemic. Our Pantry and More program was in its infancy. But when I think about how wide Rayma's door swings open now and the depth of our involvement in her life, I'm pretty much in awe.

I remember our trip to the North Carolina coast where she and two others were chauffeured by us in beach wheelchairs and treated to a seafood meal overlooking the ocean. Or how our staff and volunteers help with a wide variety of situations around her apartment, including navigating the technology it takes to pay her rent now that the leasing company no longer accepts checks. I love the photo of Rayma at our Treasure the Classics event where her head is thrown back in laughter and her arms are circled around Tammy and Janna from our EOC staff. I would say she feels loved, valued, and cared for. What a difference from that initial grocery delivery!

What changed? Perhaps it's this: help opened the door that allowed hope to come in.

In North Carolina that help may come when a volunteer delivers groceries at the end of the month when our Pantry and More clients are running low on resources.

Or when assistance arrives with the Helping Hands ministry group who may build a ramp or shore up sagging porch railings or any number of other tasks that make our older friends safer in their homes.

Perhaps we can provide a ride to a doctor's appointment for someone who doesn't drive and cannot, for a variety of reasons, use other forms of transportation.

In Romania it might have begun when a team member from the US helped an older friend with limited dexterity peel our gift of a banana—such a treat!

Or maybe help arrives when the only ink pen a Romanian friend owns runs dry and then he sees the four-color ink pen clipped on the cuff of his Christmas Stocking of Joy!

I could list a dozen more examples of times that help (practical forms of assistance) has opened the door for hope (renewed excitement about life, a sense of purpose, or a reason to get up) to come into the lives of the older friends we love and serve.

Help opens the door.

Hope comes in.

Thank you, Lord!

Prayer

Dear God, I am grateful for your faithfulness in providing both help and hope in my life. Is there a specific way you'd like to use me to be a conduit for help and hope to flow to others?

Our Complex Kitchen Complex

Suppose one of you wants to build a tower.
Won't you first sit down and estimate the cost
to see if you have enough money to complete it?
Luke 14:28

Have you ever had a plan that looked fantastic on paper?

That is, until reality hit?

Our kitchen complex project in Romania falls in that category. It's a venture that has become complex—as in *more complicated*—than we could have imagined. It's a well-planned project which in "normal times" would have been completed by now, right on schedule and within our original allocation of funds.

Our ministry partners, Mircea and Dana, did their due diligence by creating a budget and a timeline, then asked for and received bids and estimates on the work and the appliances that will be needed. We communicated frequently with them and prayerfully decided to move forward. We were thrilled when generous donors invested in this much-needed project.

It was exciting to imagine the completed complex, which will provide a large, clean, and efficient area for preparing meals not only for our friends living in elder care homes, but also for church events and for those in a nearby homeless shelter. It will allow for canning vegetables, jams, and one of my favorites: eggplant spread. There's been discussion about a possible catering side business with the purpose of bringing in funds to help the main ministry of caring for our older friends.

The plan included building onto an existing structure situated on a farm property where chickens and pigs are raised and a greenhouse already stands. What a great idea!

All this was before the cost of lumber, windows, doors—well, everything—skyrocketed, or in some cases, were simply unavailable. Workers became increasingly difficult to find and hire. There seemed to be an uptick in inspections, which added to the expense.

We've battled discouragement, prayed for guidance, and pressed on as God has provided through those who believe the project will be completed and put to its intended use. But when will that be?

Should we give up? Call it quits and count our losses?

I don't think so. When Janna, Ellen, and I traveled to Romania in November 2022, we had a powerful time of praise and prayer inside the complex building with Dana and Mircea. We walked through the building, rejoicing at all that has been completed: structure, roof, electricity, water, sewage . . . so much done. But no windows or doors. As Ellen began our time of prayer, a dove suddenly flew in, nearly landing on her head!

It was one of those you-had-to-be-there moments, but those of us who *were* there believe God was communicating. We sensed it was a "Don't give up!" memo delivered by a flying messenger.

So we moved forward. Donors felt led to purchase the windows and doors, and I'm grateful to report that the kitchen complex was airtight before winter. Beyond that, tiles have been laid.

Next comes more finishing work and acquiring needed equipment, like the uniquely translated "potato robot" (electric peeler) and everything else needed to set up a commercial kitchen. Given the state of the world, you won't be surprised to hear that prices are now much higher than our original projections.

I've talked with other ministry leaders who have projects that have stalled for similar reasons. They share my unease, bordering on embarrassment, in telling donors and other interested parties where we are in this long, drawn-out process.

I am going to continue praying and planning, but also counting the cost. I long for the day that the kitchen complex will be finished and functioning, and we will give glory to God, the giver of all good gifts.

Prayer

Dear Lord, I thank you for how you work through, both in and sometime despite the plans I make. I ask you to direct my every thought and action. May you be glorified in everything!

God the Great Connector

And may the Master pour on the love
so it fills your lives and splashes over
on everyone around you, just as it does from us to you.
1 Thessalonians 3:12 (MSG)

Once upon a time, Vince, new to town, sat down next to Justin at a local gathering spot.

They started a conversation. Vince had taken a new job with the local White Sox baseball affiliate, the Cannon Ballers. Justin loves all things baseball, coaches his son's team, and confessed that he thought Vince had a dream job! A friendship began.

I was introduced to Justin through Emily, who was one of our EOC board members at the time. Our first meeting was full of stories, laughter, and shared struggles. Our friendship continues to grow and Justin's encouragement of me and Elder Orphan Care is a huge blessing.

One summer evening my friend Janna, also an EOC staff person, and I took Janice to a Cannon Ballers game. It was the first baseball game Janice, age 74, had ever attended! She was tickled to be there, and it was a ton of fun to enjoy the experience through her eyes. I happened to run into Justin on my way to the concession stand. I told him we had an EOC friend with us. I was delighted when Justin came to where we were seated to meet Janice.

Justin, swept up in Janice's excitement to be at her first ever baseball game, said, "Janice, I'm going to tell my son to get you a game ball. He gets foul balls all the time."

And sure enough, a couple of innings later, here comes Justin, his wife Nicole, daughter Madelyn, and son Marcus, who was grinning and holding a baseball which he presented to one very thrilled Janice!

Later in the game, Justin returned with his friend Vince. We enjoyed a good visit during the in-between moments of cheering on the hometown team. Of course, Janice proudly showed him her treasured baseball. Only later did we discover that Vince is the assistant general manager of the Cannon Ballers!

Six months later, during an EOC staff meeting, Tammy reported, "I still haven't found the right person to get us connected to the Cannon Ballers to help us set up a fundraiser."

She had said that before, but suddenly it hit me. *I may know the right person!* I quickly texted Justin and sent him the photo I had taken of him, Vince, Janna, and Janice at the ball game. I explained the situation and asked if he might connect us with Vince. Within ten minutes Justin texted, "I will make an introduction with Vince. I'll text both of you together." And he did.

Vince *was* the connection we needed! After we shared our ideas about an EOC partnership with the team, Vince made the next connection with his colleague Brooke, and *boom!* Elder Orphan Care night with the Cannon Ballers at Atrium Health Ballpark is on the calendar!

Did you catch all that? All the people who started conversations, made introductions, sat to visit, went the extra mile, followed through . . . I love how God works!

It reminds me of a statement my friend Matt made when we were on a mission trip together. As our team sat in a large circle, he challenged us:

Look around you. A year, five years, or ten years from now, you may think back on this day and realize, "That was the moment it started! That was the place/person/ conversation/idea where God birthed what's happening in my life right now!" Friends, pay attention to the people around you. Make time for them. You may think they are in your life for a certain reason, or a certain season. God may have other, much more incredible ideas. One day you'll look back and say, "That's the moment it began."

Prayer

Dear God, I thank you for the ripple effects you put in motion through meetings, conversations, and friendships. Don't let me miss anything you have planned, whether I think it is important at the moment or not!

Quick to Listen

My dear brothers and sisters, take note of this:
Everyone should be quick to listen,
slow to speak and slow to become angry,
James 1:19

Is that the order you usually roll? (1) Quick to listen; (2) slow to speak? Does that describe your communication style?

You decide for yourself . . . I know *my* answer.

But, as I have tried to train myself to be a ready listener and harness my desire to speak (or interrupt), the blessings and benefits have been abundant.

When I am intentionally listening—asking questions, holding my tongue—I learn so much about our older friends, both the stories of their lives before I had the privilege of meeting them and the things they value now.

For example, among our older friends in North Carolina and Romania we have those who:

- Competed on the first women's water ski team in New Zealand

- Served as a nurse in the US Army

- Traveled to Ukraine on a mission trip

- Marched with Martin Luther King, Jr.

- Ministered to inner city New York gangs with David Wilkerson

- Served in Vietnam

- Taught Sunday school for fifty years

- Packed supplies for teams traveling to Haiti and got to travel there herself one year

- Endured unimaginable evil

- Raised children with special needs

- Lived on the streets for eight years

- Toured Israel

- Retired from successful careers

- Lived through decades of communism

- Played the trumpet in a professional jazz band

- Risked his life while distributing Bibles in underground churches

- Served as a lieutenant colonel in the Romanian army

- Survived a life-threatening illness, and now serves as a caregiver in the place where she was saved

- Watched the Lord transform the life of an eighty-year-old friend to the degree that he became a Christian too

- Had to be lowered into the baptistry with ropes because he has no legs

- Is raising the teenage daughter of a friend who died

I am touched by what our friend Ema in Romania says about members of our teams from the US who spend time with the elders there: "What you do, most do not: you sit and visit and listen, touch, and hug. The elders here consider you more than friends, you are family."

Ema's insights made me wonder.

What if one way God "sets the lonely in families" (Psalm 68:6) is when we listen?

What if listening is a vital component of how we "show respect for the elderly" as we are instructed to do in Leviticus 19:32?

Whether I'm right about those verses or not, I am sure of this: God has equipped all of us with what it takes to love others with our ears.

Prayer

*Dear God, listening can be both easy and difficult.
Please teach me to listen in ways that reflects
your compassion for those around me.*

Hope Springs Eternal

*Now faith is confidence in what we hope for
and assurance about what we do not see.
Hebrews 11:1*

Elder Orphan Care has been abundantly blessed to have Emily Evans serve with us as a social work intern as part of her master's program. I can't begin to communicate the depth of knowledge and experience Emily has brought to us. She's been an invaluable help to our North Carolina clients and has become a good friend to each of us on staff. We've learned so much from her, and as you will read in her words that follow, it would seem that EOC has impacted her as well.

As a social worker for nearly twenty years, I have been trained to assess an individual's needs, identify potential resources to help, and connect them to these resources. I have operated under the assumption that the reason for individual suffering is the lack of access to a needed resource—and, by helping to provide that resource, suffering could be alleviated.

Having the opportunity to intern with EOC has shown me that this is only part of the equation. The mission statement of EOC is to provide help and hope for older adults in need, specifically those aging alone. Help comes in practical forms; hope comes through Jesus Christ. The stories in *Hello, Hope!* allow us to reflect on our past "Yay, God!" moments, as Kim would be keen to say, and lead us to positive expectations for the future.

There are numerous needs that can impact an individual's health and wellbeing, such as financial, transportation, housing, nutritional, medical, environmental safety, and relationships. EOC's older adults face many, if not all, of these needs. However, it is not enough to meet the practical needs if we fail to address the underlying emotional needs. Hope instills the initiative and motivation necessary for positive change.

Research indicates that having hope improves mental health, reduces depression and anxiety, improves coping with illness, and increases meaning, purpose, and life satisfaction. Spending time with the EOC staff and clients has taught me what a valuable resource we all have at our disposal, should we choose to accept it. Hope is not a finite resource which we have to hoard in case it runs out. As the famous poet Alexander Pope reminds us, "Hope springs eternal."

There are several hope-based strategies we can employ in daily life when our well of hope seems to run dry:

- **Emphasize strengths**, focusing on what we can do instead of what we can't.

- **Practice hopeful thinking**, envisioning a future when we achieve our desired outcome. Notice this takes *practice*, meaning the more we try this the easier it will become.

- **Surround ourselves with hopeful and optimistic people.** I can attest to this through spending time with Kim, Janna, and Tammy over the past year. Their optimism is contagious!

- **Engage in gratitude**, whether through reflection, journaling, or writing thank-you notes. Gratitude can generate feelings of hopefulness for the future.

- **Discover a sense of purpose**. Purpose helps us cope with stress and find strength amid crisis. Often this purpose is connected to community, cultivating spirituality, and participating in meaningful activities. Working closely with EOC's amazing occupational therapy-minded staff has shown me just how important this last point is. They are so good at identifying what is meaningful to an individual and finding creative ways to allow them to do more of it.

Regardless of where my future career and life take me, I intend to never underestimate the power of *hope* in someone's life. As a believer in Christ, I understand that God is the ultimate source of my hope and take comfort in the eternal nature of this hope. I can view suffering through a lens of expectation, waiting for the next "Yay, God!" moment to build resilience for the future.

Prayer

Dear God, I thank you for hope. Because you are its source, it is indeed unlimited and eternal. Please show me how to nurture your gift of hope.

Handmade and from the Heart

He has filled them with skill to do every sort of work done by
an engraver or by a designer or by an embroiderer
in blue and purple and scarlet yarns and fine twined linen,
or by a weaver—by any sort of workman or skilled designer.
Exodus 35:35 (ESV)

Silviya, a new friend from the Romanian Baptist Church in Charlotte, approached me after I spoke there and asked if we could use Christmas cards for our annual Stockings of Joy project. I told her we sure could, but we needed quite a few.

"How many is that?"

"We need 500 for Romania and 330 locally."

"OK," she replied, not batting an eye. "I'll be in touch."

I could hardly believe it the day she handed me two heavy bags containing 830 hand-stamped cards she and her five children, aged two to twelve, had made! So many cards! You know that type of service comes from the heart!

As does this: Melanie bakes fifty mini pound cakes each December to be included with the holiday meal our volunteers deliver to our North Carolina older friends, whose eyes light up when they see that treat!

EOC is abundantly blessed with a host of knitters, crocheters, quilters, and sewists (those who sew). I think of Pam who encouraged her Stitching Souls group to crochet hundreds of soap cozies and red-and-white candy cane ornaments to include in our Stockings of Joy. Or Karen, whose quilted creations bless our Romanian friends, or the Cabarrus Quilters Guild, whose donations grace some of the homes of our local clients.

What would we do without individuals and groups in Missouri, Illinois, Indiana, Ohio, Montana, Virginia, and North Carolina who so faithfully make 1,000 Christmas Stockings and Tote Bags of Joy each year? Amy and her crew at Roseville Christian

Church routinely make one hundred stockings, and two other groups—Stitch 'n Go in Springfield, Illinois, and Sew, Quilt, Share in Findlay, Ohio—each create over 300 stockings every year!

We are grateful for Vickie and the prayer shawl ministry she leads in Concord, North Carolina. Each October Vickie delivers huge bags of colorful scarves and shawls lovingly made by her group. I so appreciate the photograph she sent me showing dozens of their handiwork creations hanging over the altar rails at Central United Methodist Church where members prayed over them before Vickie brought them to us. Just imagine how the work of their hands is providing comfort to our older friends in Romania and Ukraine!

We praise God for young Mackenzie who crochets wash cloths, prays over them, and adds a special note of encouragement before donating them to EOC. And we thank the Lord for our You Are Remembered volunteers who send cards, often handmade, from their homes in Indiana or New Mexico to our North Carolina clients. Here's a statement that sums up how those cards are valued: "I can't display them all because I receive so many, but I certainly can't throw them away. So I've put them all in a notebook and I look through it and enjoy the cards again and again."

Thanks to EOC staff member Janna telling her friend Pam in Missouri all about EOC, a mini-Elder Orphan Care has begun there! Pam not only organized a group of friends to make tote bags for us, but her church life group has also adopted older friends in an elder care home in their area and are sharing God's love with them. They even developed their own Christmas Stockings of Joy program!

And what can I say about Suzanne and all our friends in the Loving Hearts Sewing Circle? They continue to amaze us with their masterpiece designs which have included pillowcases, embroidered gifts, beautiful and useful zippered bags, heart-shaped pillows, and Easter baskets created from kitty litter containers! Our North Carolina clients can hardly wait to see what they'll come up with next!

Board member Ellen is our connection with the creative Common Thread ministry from Lakeview Wesleyan Church in Indiana. Her cousins, who are active in that group, became interested in EOC when Ellen shared about it on Facebook. Since then they have been making colorful hats and scarves that are big blessings for our Romanian friends.

I love the enthusiasm of the Stitch 'n Go group in Springfield, Illinois. When they heard that last year we came up shy of the 600 handmade hats we needed and consequently had to purchase some, their immediate response was, "That won't happen again," and sprang into action! I am confident that *all* of our winter hats will be handmade this year!

Obviously EOC could purchase Christmas stockings, winter hats, warm scarves, cards, and everything else we give to our older friends, but don't you agree that there's just something special about handmade and from the heart?

Prayer

Dear Lord, I know you are Creator God, and I am made in your image, so there's no doubt that I have some sort of creative gift, whether it's artistic or innovative. Please show me how to use the skills and gifts you have deposited in me for your glory and the good of others.

Poor of Pocketbook or Poor of Spirit

Be sure to welcome strangers into your home.
By doing this, some people have welcomed angels
as guests, without even knowing it.
Hebrews 13:2 (CEV)

All of our older friends in Romania are impoverished. In North Carolina, most of our clients, who are sixty or older, fall at least 150% below the federal poverty level.

Here's a story that will make that statement more understandable. When EOC staff members Janna and Emily helped a new client fill out our application they discovered she makes $820 per month working at a fast-food restaurant. Her rent is $530. She hadn't been to see a doctor in two years. Her blood pressure was off the charts. She needed medical equipment she couldn't afford.

Janna got her an appointment with a doctor, took her to it, and served as an advocate. We provided the needed adaptive equipment. She was enrolled in a program to receive free medicines and we signed her up for our Pantry and More program. When she saw the grocery list, she began to weep. "You're going to get all this good food for me? I can't believe it!"

There is no doubt that this dear soul is poor of pocketbook.

But we also have clients who have sufficient financial resources, at least for now. But they are lonely. Isolated. Often discouraged, sometimes overwhelmed. In some cases, grieving. These precious folks are what I term *poor of spirit*.

I cannot speak to this personally, but after a presentation where I had shared about the work of Elder Orphan Care, a very wise woman took the time to write me with her personal insights, which are powerful. Here are excerpts from that letter:

First, there are many elder orphans like me who are not impoverished for daily needs and are blessed to be able to provide for themselves. However, they may be impoverished in spirit, live in loneliness, see that their friends have predeceased them or moved away, and suffer, especially during holidays. Their children may have turned the corner into lives of their own and seldom renew relations with parents. Unfortunately, the world identifies needs based on the metric of "low income," but other needs may be just as great.

Secondly, I am an elder orphan who lives in a world of couples. Singles do not, in my experience, get invitations into homes and especially not on holidays. They have to buddy with each other. This presents another dimension to your ministry! Why do Christian couples and families not include aged people who are single at their table for holiday dinners? Where I live, a civic club picks up the people who are alone or are not invited into a home for holidays and provides meals for them in a community setting.

I remember my younger days raising a family when there was always room for another plate on the table and we usually scooped up the children's music teachers who gave them private lessons if they had nowhere to go. My parents would invite my aunt, who was not an aunt at all but lived alone "on relief." Dad even took his car out of the garage and picked her up in his vehicle to make her queen for a day.

So I leave you with the idea about hospitality for elder orphans, whether financial-needy or fellowship-needy, as a dimension of your ministry.

Prayer

Dear God, please speak to me about what I have just read. Whether I live alone or am surrounded by family, have resources to share or need them, I ask you to reveal your heart to me.

Lasting Legacy

*Generation after generation stands in awe of your work; each
one tells stories of your mighty acts.*
Psalm 145:4 (MSG)

When my position at an assisted living community was
eliminated and I became instantly unemployed, I emailed
a mentor of mine to tell her the news. For months I had been
asking God for his wisdom regarding the next season of my life,
so I was certain he was going to use this surprise for his glory.
Ellen strengthened my conviction with this response:

"Kingdom living is high adventure, isn't it? I look forward to your
next assignment!"

Ellen and I originally met through a class my friend Cathi
and I taught called the "Creative Heart of God." Ellen was an
artist of note but far more importantly she was a beloved sister
in Christ and a champion of the gospel. She was the prayer
warrior you wanted in your corner. She opened her heart and
her home to friends and strangers. Her smile was breathtaking
and nearly constant, and she lived with a profound joy; she
was humble; she was an encourager.

She continued to minister to those around her even as she was
facing her own death, encouraging one visitor, "Don't be sad. I'm
not."

Ellen is one of many people of faith who have impacted my life by
their words and deeds. Here are some others:

- Frank once confided a deep desire of his heart. "I'd like to
  write my last check to a missionary and die broke."

- As I began to write this third volume of *Hello, Hope!* I
  came across a note from JoAnn, a dear friend and former
  EOC board member who was a teammate on two trips to
  Romania. Her encouragement means even more to me now
  that she has relocated from earth to be with the Lord: "Kim, I
  am really enjoying *Hello, Hope!* I am SO proud of you! I would

like to buy ten more copies to give to my Bible study group. Thanks, my friend, for being you!"

- I love what Twila wrote in a note she included with a special donation: "I am honored to send this gift in memory of Pat Syester. Though we never met, she inspired many people whom I love. The testimony of her life has a far reach—even to me."

- We can only praise God when made aware that someone is so convinced of God's work through Elder Orphan Care that they determine to include EOC in their financial legacy, allowing their generosity to continue beyond their earthly days!

- When my friend Cathi visits her older friend in a nursing home, staff members frequently mistake her as Del's daughter. She's not—no relation at all—but has taken on the very important and sometimes difficult role of caring for this woman with whom she shares a rich history.

- I am in awe of the decision that Susan and her husband made early in their marriage. They both had jobs, so they determined to live on his salary and give her salary to missions. Just imagine their investment in eternity!

- I could write an entire book about my mom, Doris Rose Bush Jackson, and I may someday. It's difficult to imagine she's been gone since 1999, especially because her life continues to affect mine so greatly. She taught me so much about perseverance and perspective, not so much by what she said, but by how she lived. But her words impacted me, too, and these that she wrote inside a set of reference books, a Christmas gift to me when I was thirty-two, continue to encourage me three decades later:

Dear Daughter Kim,

I thought these five slim volumes might help you as you continue to develop your writing and speaking career. You know you don't have to be a Nobel prize winner for me to think you are the greatest. I already do. God bless and be with you all your life and in all your endeavors. Remember I love you and always will.

Mom

I pray that these examples have caused you to consider or reconsider what you will leave behind once your life on earth is over. Perhaps these challenges will also inspire you:

- Pray without ceasing, for prayers spoken now will outlive you!

- Ponder this statement by Randy Alcorn, "What you do with your resources in this life is your autobiography." [2]

- Put your testimony stories in some form that will outlast your days on earth.

- Personalize and give meaningful gifts.

- Prioritize the days of your life in light of eternity.

- Praise the Lord every chance you get; make it a habit to brag on God!

- Pursue a life lived by faith and not by sight.

- Persevere in the power God provides.

Prayer

Dear God, first and foremost, I want to make you famous! And in so doing, I want to leave a legacy that can only be explained in the context of my relationship with you, Jesus.

2; Randy Alcorn, *Money, Possessions, and Eternity* (Carol Stream, IL: Tyndale House Publishers, 2003),152.

Wondering How God Might Use Me

*People should tell about the good things she has done: raising
children, being hospitable, taking care of believers' needs,
helping the suffering, or always doing good things.*
1 Timothy 5:10 (GW)

My friend Janna, who is EOC's Director of Community Programs,
had a twenty-year career as a professional nanny before deciding
to return to school at age forty to get her master's degree in
occupational therapy.

St. Ambrose University was about an hour and a half drive
from her home, so it was too far to commute to classes, but
she didn't want to go to the expense of renting an apartment.
She remembered a friend from years past whose sister lived in
Davenport, Iowa, where St. Ambrose is located, so Janna got
the sister's contact information and called her.

"Do you happen to know of anyone who would want to rent a
room to a nontraditional student?"

Linda had a great idea. "I'll go to my church's senior adult
Sunday school class and ask if any of them might be interested."

And that was the beginning of a beautiful story of shared
experiences, boomerang blessings, powerful purposes, and
intergenerational friendship. Here is that story in Janna's words:

> Della, a lively eighty-three-year-old woman, was in the
> class the Sunday Linda presented my request. She was
> a widow and recently had cared for her sister-in-law until
> she died. That left quite a void in her life and Della was
> wondering how God might use her next. She had already
> scoured neighborhood yard sales rounding up unwanted
> sewing machines, put them in her basement, and recruited
> her friends to come every Tuesday to make diapers from
> towels to be sent to an orphanage in Haiti. But she was
> wondering what other ways God might use her.
>
> When she heard a college student needed a place to stay,

she jumped at the chance to open her home.

Della and I met for lunch and immediately hit it off. Afterwards I went to her home for a tour, and when August came, I moved into her extra bedroom. She even fixed up another room for me to use as an office for studying.

I lived with Della for three years. She would never allow me to pay her. Not only that, but she fixed me breakfast every morning and handed me a bag lunch when I left for classes.

She would have supper ready when I returned. Then we'd watch her favorite TV show, after which she would say, "It's time for you to study." Each evening at 10:00 p.m. she knocked on the door and said, "Time for bed." If I replied that I wasn't done studying, she would say, "You've done all the learning you can for today."

Della became our occupational therapy class adopted grandma. She loved going to class with me if we needed a "guinea pig" to do manual muscle testing or transfer training.

She would host my study group at her home—and provided snacks, of course! She became friends with my parents, who were her peers, and would sometimes go home with me on weekends.

We grew to love one another deeply; in fact, we became family. It was such a wonderful setup for both of us: she had purpose and was no longer isolated, and I had a place to stay and a wonderful friend who provided not only a home but the structure I needed. I learned so much from Della about life, faith, and cooking!

When I received my master's degree, my parents gave Della a graduation card too! She had been with me every step of the way. She was undoubtedly an honorary occupational therapist.

We stayed in touch after I moved to North Carolina and

I made it a point to visit her in Iowa whenever I could. Della is with the Lord now but her influence in my life remains. I will be forever grateful that at age eighty-three she wondered what God might have for her to do next, and that a student named Janna was his answer!

Prayer

Dear God, I thank you for everyone you use to bring your good gifts into my life. I want to be a conduit of blessing to others, too! How would you like to use me?

Love Always Fits

So, chosen by God for this new life of love,
dress in the wardrobe God picked out for you:
compassion, kindness, humility, quiet strength, discipline.
Colossians 3:12 (MSG)

I didn't mean to eavesdrop. I just couldn't help but overhear what they were saying.

The three silver-haired ladies were at the dress rack next to the clearance items I was perusing. Their conversation began innocently.

"Oh Mildred, you would look good in this," commented Lady Number One, as she held up a modest green dress.

Lady Number Two agreed, "Oh my, yes."

Mildred, who seemed to hold the trio's seniority, responded, "Well, now, it's interesting you'd say that. I already have a dress in that same style, only it's blue."

Ladies Number One and Two smiled and nodded in tandem.

Mildred continued, "I'm going to be buried in it."

I'll admit it was at this point that I began to full-on eavesdrop. And I'm glad I did. I would have hated to miss what came next.

"I'll have to lose a little weight first," Mildred concluded.

My brain desperately tried to comprehend what I'd just heard: this sweet little lady has to lose weight before she can die? Now this is merely my humble opinion, but I think we're getting into a weird area when you have to diet before you can die. Surely there's a simpler solution: elastic, perhaps?

Still, there is something to be said for preparing to meet your Maker. The Bible gives great counsel in that regard, but as far as I can tell, none of it has to do with scales or fashion.

Unless you consider the believer's pre-burial wardrobe, as outlined in Colossians 3:12–14:

> Therefore, as God's chosen people, holy and dearly loved, clothe yourselves with compassion, kindness, humility, gentleness and patience. Bear with each other and forgive one another if any of you has a grievance against someone. Forgive as the Lord forgave you. And over all these virtues put on love, which binds them all together in perfect unity.

I don't know if Mildred is still alive, or if her body has been laid to rest in her (tight?) blue dress. What I do know is that each of us will one day be called into God's glorious presence, where the perishable will be clothed with the imperishable, according to 1 Corinthians 15:53-54. Until that moment, we can choose to wear love.

And love always fits.

Prayer

Dear God, you are love by definition
(1 John 4:8) and in Scripture you say that believers
will be known by how we love (John 13:35).
Lord, I need your power within me to love well.

Sovereign Spiritipity

From the beginning I revealed the end. From long ago
I told you things that had not yet happened, saying,
"My plan will stand, and I'll do everything I intended to do."
Isaiah 46:10 (GW)

To this day Alisa doesn't know how a post from the Elder Orphan Care Facebook page appeared in her newsfeed.

But I do. It was what I call "Sovereign Spiritipity." The word *sovereign* means "possessing supreme power." *Spiritipity*, a word I coined, describes how God's Spirit creatively orchestrates events or circumstances in ways far beyond human comprehension.

When Alisa saw the EOC Facebook post, it resonated with her. The Scripture verse spoke to her heart, and she was compelled to contact us. She messaged Elder Orphan Care, I replied, and that began our long-distance friendship. Over the years we have shared many joys and heartaches. We encourage one another. She supports EOC financially and with her prayers.

I have learned so much from Alisa. She has a unique voice.

Alisa can speak to the situation of older adults who find themselves aging alone from a variety of angles.

She was an elder care lawyer. The theme of her thirty-year legal career was Isaiah 1:17: "Learn to do right; seek justice. Defend the oppressed. Take up the cause of the fatherless; plead the case of the widow."

That verse defined her professional life. Her personal life ran a parallel track. Over many years, Alisa cared for her father, her mother, and her brother, all who faced a variety of medical challenges, until they passed from this life.

Now she says, "I am the elder orphan I once defended, supported, and helped. I am the family member in need of assistance . . . but the difference is, I have no family."

Alisa understands all too well the myriad challenges of aging without adequate support. Several of those issues came to a head when she underwent reconstructive surgery after a failed knee replacement and was faced with navigating all the resulting problems.

Alisa can also speak from the perspective of a church member.

When her church began the process of building an addition, Alisa met with her pastor to encourage him to remember the needs of older members as the new facility was constructed. Unbelievably his response was, "We are going after the younger generation these days."

Alisa's experience, while not universal, has been that churches tend to focus on families or the young. She says, "A single senior like me is invisible." She continues, "God promised in Psalm 68:6 to 'put the solitary in families,' but I am still waiting for mine. Perhaps it is simply a promise that will not be fulfilled this side of heaven."

Amid her own health issues and other challenges, Alisa dreams of starting an Elder Orphan Care of sorts in her area.

> Starting an EOC ministry is something that I barely whisper to God. I can hardly take care of myself. So how in the world could I help extend your ministry here? But I always preferred older people. Even as a young girl, I wanted to sit and talk to them.

> I was an elder law attorney. I regulated nursing homes. Older people have my heart. And now the burden I feel growing is to help others like me, who are elder orphans.

I don't know what God has planned for Alisa, me, and EOC in the days to come. But I'm confident he's up to something amazing. I'm grateful that his plans are so important, so near to his great heart, that he used a social media post to Spiritipitously connect Alisa and me across 865 miles!

Prayer

*Dear God, I thank you for how you creatively
bring people together for your glory and our good.
Please reveal to me any connections I may have
overlooked, or ones that you would like to deepen.*

Someone You've Never Met
Is Looking Out for You

All praise to God, the Father of our Lord Jesus Christ.
God is our merciful Father and the source of all comfort.
He comforts us in all our troubles so that we can comfort
others. When they are troubled, we will be able to give
them the same comfort God has given us.
2 Corinthians 1:3-4 (NLT)

By age fifty-eight my right knee had had enough. Perhaps all those years of being a softball catcher caught up with me. Whatever the reason, it was frequently so swollen and painful that I had to sort of drag it along behind me. It was time to get a new knee.

I lived in a second-floor apartment with no elevator. My friend JoAnn invited me to stay in her home after my knee replacement surgery in a ground-level bedroom she had made accessible for her mom while she lived with her. What a gift! I don't know what I would have done otherwise.

That was one of many lessons I learned from my bum knee and the ensuing surgery, therapy, and recovery: the world we live in often isn't designed for people with physical limitations.

For example, I understand that there are reasons behind the fact that most toilets sit fifteen inches off the ground. Inquiring minds can google to discover the rationale. But the logic is not all that helpful when your bad knee will no longer cooperate in the "help-me-get-up-off-this-thing" process.

Those of you who have experienced that panic will appreciate someone named Patricia Moore. I've never met her, but I've benefited from her wisdom, and it's a good bet you have too.

When Patricia began her career in the 1970s, she was the only female out of 350 employees working in product development at a prestigious industrial design company in New York. Consequently, as she puts it, "I was the uncommon voice."

She had the courage to ask questions like, "Why wouldn't we think about people who suffer from arthritis when we design a refrigerator door or a can opener?" and "What about people who don't have feet to walk with and use wheels instead?"

The response she received was always, "Patricia, we don't design for those people."

But Patricia believed that design should empower people, not disable them. She couldn't come to grips with the mindset that some people deserved good design and others didn't. So she launched a bold experiment. Patricia, at age twenty-six, became an eighty-five-year-old woman. She wore a prosthetic cocoon that mimicked curvature of the spine; glasses with cloudy lenses, a silver wig, hearing aids, and shoes that altered her gait. She used a walker, a wheelchair, or a cane to create different levels of reduced mobility. All with the goal of understanding the challenges someone with those conditions would face.

She immersed herself in nine different older personas, including a woman who was homeless and one who was wealthy. She quickly discovered she couldn't open doors, reach items, or read directions. She was dependent on others around her to do the simplest of tasks. She experienced a variety of emotions; was overlooked, dismissed, met with various actions and attitudes. Her story is fascinating, and the result of those years are experiences and insights that led to action. For example, if you use any of several OXO brand Good Grips kitchen utensils, you are benefiting from what Patricia Moore learned.

I'll probably never meet Patricia Moore, as much as I'd like to. But I think she would be proud of EOC, and especially Janna and Tammy, who so frequently use their occupational therapy skills and knowledge to make life better for our older friends.

If I'd had my way, my original right knee would have lasted my lifetime. But I am grateful to God that since it didn't, I got a new one. And I believe that God never wastes experiences. He will use every pain if we offer it to him. Because I have a six-inch scar over my right kneecap, I have more sensitivity to those God has called me to serve.

What painful experience have you endured that God may use to help someone else?

Prayer

Dear God, I thank you for people who not only empathize with those who face challenges in navigating the world but who also take action to help them overcome the obstacles.

Volunteers Extraordinaire

Do not withhold good from those to whom it is due,
when it is in your power to act.
Proverbs 3:27

Gene, who's an EOC volunteer in North Carolina along with his wife, called with this update: "Deb and I got groceries for the girls today and Alma's next appointment is March 25, so we'll take her again, and we're picking Rosie up for church Sunday."

I love everything about that phone call. For one thing, "the girls" are seventy-five and seventy-nine years old! I love Gene's term of endearment, and they do too.

I can't begin to brag on every volunteer who helps with our North Carolina outreach, and honestly, they wouldn't want me to. But here are few examples of our volunteers extraordinaire:

- One of our youngest volunteers is three years old. My favorite Tobias story is the time he picked a bowl of blueberries for ninety-year-old Edna after he and his parents delivered her groceries.

- Our oldest volunteer, Jean, is ninety-two. I can still see her in the Christmas Tote Bags of Joy assembly line, helping pack gifts for 330 people, most of whom are younger than she is!

- When Krista delivered Rayma's air fryer Christmas gift, she unpacked it and helped her learn to make a favorite snack—french fries. Olivia did a similar kindness when she not only took Alma's new light vacuum to her apartment, but also put it together, taught her how to use it, and carried the empty box out to the dumpster.

- Each year our Christmas Wish List program has grown both in size and in special touches. The first year, three of us met in a home and did well to put a couple of dozen unwrapped gifts in bags with tissue paper. Most recently we met in a gymnasium where volunteers gathered to beautifully wrap over two hundred gifts. Our friend Lori spent hours adding her elegant, handcrafted bows.

- I could write several pages bragging on our Helping Hands volunteers who do all types of home modification projects to help keep our older friends safe. These hardworking, fun-loving men include several veterans and retirees as well as young men who sometimes bring their children along. They offer not only amazing skill sets, but huge hearts of compassion. I know without a doubt that God has some very special rewards awaiting Ray, Jack, Dan, Greg, Dick, Jason, Shawn, and everyone who lends a literal hand to help!

- Tim, another home modification volunteer who often works solo, doesn't even live in either of the North Carolina counties we serve, but chooses to drive the distance to use his skills to benefit our clients.

- Karen, a retired RN, not only serves through providing transportation to doctor's appointments, but is a trusted medical advocate for those who have no one to help them navigate the often-confusing world of health care.

- We are so grateful for our EOC volunteers who shop each month for healthy and fresh foods for our clients. And the cashiers at the grocery store have unexpectedly become important volunteers as well! Brigitte, Cathy, and others enthusiastically assist us by packing groceries in color-specific bags and then go the extra mile by weighing each bag for us, which is a requirement for our grant reports.

- Pastor Shawn and Kimberly and friends from BLVD Chapel are fun and creative volunteers. Whether leading our Easter caroling event or preparing crafts and serving refreshments at our Summer Celebration, they joyfully share the love of God.

- Our faithful You are Remembered group of eight women has been sending love through the mail to our North Carolina clients from Indiana and Florida for several years. As the number of our clients has grown, we saw a need to expand this program. Janna recruited her friend Gloria, and Gloria asked friends to help. Now they mail encouraging cards to our grateful clients in North Carolina from New Mexico!

We have three volunteers who share the same first name. I call them our Super Sandys!

- Sandy H calls to get our clients' grocery lists. Then she listens for a lot longer than it takes to write down what they need. After she shops for Larry's groceries, she picks up his favorite meal and delivers that, too. Sandy takes time to visit and pray. One day Larry mentioned that "Mansion Over the Hilltop" was his favorite hymn. Sandy surprised him by singing it, and he joined in. Sandy told me "It seems that singing was just what he needed that day."

- Sandy P is one of our long-time EOC buddies who goes above and beyond in her care for Kathy. It's not always easy. She takes a lot of phone calls and handles more than a few challenging, and sometimes unusual scenarios. I love it when Sandy let us know that she took "our gal" out for lunch and shopping or we find out she's invited Kathy to her home for a holiday event.

- Sandy B shops for and delivers groceries to several clients each month. Sandy volunteered to pick up one of our older friends so she could attend a special event and when they arrived I realized with gratitude that Sandy had transported not only our new client but had loaded up a host of her necessary medical equipment as well.

The dictionary defines the word *extraordinaire* as "outstanding or remarkable." Yes! That describes our volunteers perfectly!

Prayer

Dear God, I thank you for providing so many wonderful volunteers who serve with Elder Orphan Care. Please continue to provide every volunteer they need to do all you ask them to do. Direct me toward any new or different ways you may be calling me to serve my older neighbors.

God Will Provide

So Abraham called that place The Lord Will Provide.
Genesis 22:14

Our church service had overflowed into an unplanned and extended time of praise. As the final chords were played and the music faded, James, a fellow worshiper, handed me a small scrap of paper. "This is for you." It was a drawing he'd sketched on the back of a store receipt during the service.

I felt an emotional jolt when I looked at the drawing, which depicts a hand extending from above, offering a large stone to a figure laboring below who is placing similar stones together to form an expanding foundation.

My response to the drawing was, "Thank you, God, for this picture, this promise of continued provision." In my mind, it seems entirely encouraging.

When I showed it to a friend who is connected to EOC, her response was "I just wish God would give us more than one brick at a time."

Not quite as reassuring, but I certainly understand the thought.

I will admit that there are days I wonder what it would feel like if Elder Orphan Care was so completely funded that we didn't have to plan another fundraiser, apply for another grant, go on another trip to ask for new donors, post requests on social media, speak at gatherings to share our needs, ask for sponsors for events, or try to create a budget without knowing how much money will be donated or raised in the year ahead.

I hate to say it, but sometimes my faith wavers and anxiety awakens me at 3:00 a.m. I find myself fretting about grant funds that will be expended ahead of our predictions, or donors who need to reduce their level of generosity.

So that's when I begin to rehearse the faithfulness of God.

I remind myself that Elder Orphan Care was God's idea, he has sustained it so far, and it's in his hands to provide going forward. Then I encourage myself by recalling specific instances worth celebrating:

- I remember the first year of EOC's charity status when our revenue was so small that all we had to do to fulfill our tax obligation was send in a postcard to the government. Praise God, those days are long gone!

- I recall the bright yellow flags flying at each of Viorel Pasca's care homes in Romania, emblazoned with these words in red: *Dumnezeu Poarta De Grija*, which translates "God takes care." It's been Viorel's proclamation from the start, when he said to God: "I will do the work of caring for elderly who've been abandoned if you will provide the money to do it." And that is what has happened year after year. As Viorel confirms. "It's like a continuous wonder how God provides!'

- I think of two different times I was handed a $20,000 check, or the day a $25,000 check arrived in the mail "out of the blue." I will never forget my shock when I was given $10,000 in cash with the admonition, "Use this to help the poor elders in Romania."

- I still have the plastic baggie with "I can help" written on it. It contained an eight-year-old's sacrificial donation to EOC: $7.00 in scrunched up bills!

- I bring to mind the notes Alisa writes on the memo line of her checks, like "Seed for the sower" and "May God do abundantly more."

- I think of the individuals and churches who have faithfully given each month since day one of EOC, providing consistent income for what God has called us to do.

- I smile when I think of a group of older friends at a local independent living community, who determined to give an offering to EOC—and donated over $800!

- I'm thankful for all the individuals who donate through their employer's matching gift portal, so their generosity doubles!

- I remember dozens of donations made in memory of loved ones who have gone to be with the Lord.

- I recall specific emails arriving in my inbox notifying me of unexpected donations, made at just the right time.

- I think of the Crossroads Classics group whose members bring needed Pantry and More items to their meetings each month, blessing our clients and saving EOC money that can be used in other ways.

- I'm grateful for donors who send encouraging notes reminding us they are not only giving, they are praying.

My pastor, Lowell, was preaching a sermon about God's provision, when he explained what is translated "The Lord Will Provide" in Genesis 22:14 is *Jehovah-Jireh* in Hebrew. He told a story from his college days when neither he nor his friends had abundant resources. When they prayed for provision, they frequently experienced God's marvelous answers. Each time God provided they would joyfully exclaim, "Jehovah just jireh-ed!"

I love that! And certainly, there are innumerable times that I could praise God with the same chant: "Jehovah just jireh-ed!"

Sometimes I wonder how it would feel to know—be completely confident—that all EOC's financial needs will be met.

Come to think of it, I already know.

I just need to remember.

Prayer

Dear God, I praise you, Jehovah-Jireh! I acknowledge that your greatest provision is your Son, Jesus, who secured my salvation! I am grateful for every way you provide for me.

Dream Big—No, Bigger!

Now to Him Who, by (in consequence of) the [action of His]
power that is at work within us, is able to [carry out His
purpose and] do superabundantly, far over and above all that
we [dare] ask or think [infinitely beyond our highest prayers,
desires, thoughts, hopes, or dreams] . . .
Ephesians 3:20 (AMPC)

Would you do me a favor? Read Ephesians 3:20 above one
more time, slowly . . .

How do you react to those words? What impact do they have
on you? My first thought is *That's crazy!* But it's followed
quickly by *Sign me up!*

Imagine! God's mighty power is at work in the likes of me,
and you!

But wait, there's more! God is able, through his power working in
us, to do superabundantly beyond what we ask of him in prayer;
to eclipse what we are dreaming, thinking, imagining!

Isn't that completely mind-boggling?

So what's our role in bringing this Scripture to life? Here's what
I'm thinking:

- For God to deposit his power in us, we must be receptive,
  attentive, prepared vessels.

- For God to exceed our prayers, we need to give him a
  baseline to surpass!

If you're ready to take action, perhaps it's time to write something
like this in your journal, along with a list of your hopes, dreams,
and ideas: "Mighty God, I am asking you to deposit more of your
power in me to accomplish what I am asking, dreaming, and
imagining, all for your glory, Lord!"

And then, I have another favor to ask:

Would you devote time to asking God to display his power in Elder Orphan Care's staff, board, ministry partners, donors, and volunteers in ways that will exceed the big dreams we are putting before him?

I am energized by imagining hundreds of *Hello, Hope!* readers praying for God to move mightily in these areas:

- Receiving funding required to continue and expand all current programs and projects

- Securing salaries for more staff to oversee EOC's growing outreaches

- Acquiring an activity van for North Carolina

- Creating Love Your Older Neighbor curriculum resources

- Finding housing solutions for our clients in North Carolina when their homes are no longer safe

- Hiring a Director of Purpose/Activity Director for Romania

- Building a chapel in Dumbrava, Romania

- Raising funds to equip the kitchen complex in Romania

- Obtaining a building for use as EOC Central in North Carolina

Most of those requests are self-explanatory, perhaps except for our need for what we are calling EOC Central. To assist you in praying, here's the backstory:

We are grateful for all the places and spaces that we occupy, whether they are donated or rented. However, they are quite scattered! Our staff and volunteers spend precious time driving between

- Our donated office space (that we've outgrown);

- Our rented storage area that contains the medical equipment we provide;

- Our donated pantry space;

- Churches that provide larger work areas;

- Our clients' homes across two counties;

- Our UPS mailbox;

- My driveway, where the EOC grocery van is parked so the catalytic converter doesn't get stolen again!

Please hear my heart on this: we give God praise for all these scattered spaces! We simply long to be more efficient in doing the work God has for us to do.

Bottom line: If God wants to exceed what we ask for, then we need to be asking, right? Thank you for joining us in dreaming big—no, BIGGER!

Prayer

Dear God, I thank you for being a God of more.
I praise you for depositing your power in me.
I will joyfully pray, do what you ask me to do,
and then rejoice when you exceed my
expectations—all for your glory!

Connect with Elder Orphan Care

Please consider investing in Elder Orphan Care to assist us in providing help and hope for older adults who are aging without adequate support.

To make a secure online financial donation, visit:

www.elderorphancare.com

To donate by check, use our mailing address:

Elder Orphan Care
349-L Copperfield Blvd.
Suite 211
Concord, NC 28025

To receive more information, contact our staff:

Kim Jackson, Executive Director
kim.jackson@elderorphancare.com
704-787-5280

Tammy Blackburn, Director of Development
tammy.blackburn@elderorphancare.com
704-433-5779

Janna Syester, Director of Community Programs
janna.syester@elderorphancare.com
704-516-1522

Please visit *elderorphancare.com* and follow Elder Orphan Care and *Hello, Hope!* on social media for encouragement and updates.